The **Writing Twins** Present

Writing Great Dialogue

The **Writing Twins** Present

Writing Great Dialogue

Mark & Claire Stibbe

The Writing Twins Present – WRITING GREAT DIALOGUE

Copyright © 2015 by Mark & Claire Stibbe

Published by KINGDOM WRITING SOLUTIONS
Gargrave, North Yorkshire, BD23 3NG
www.kingdomwritingsolutions.org

ISBN: 978-1518808685

CONTENTS

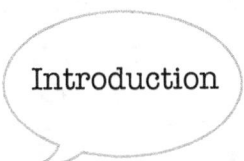

Introduction

HEAT UP YOUR DIALOGUE

Mastering the art of dialogue is one of the toughest challenges for writers of both fiction and nonfiction. It takes time to understand the differences between the way people talk in real life and in written dialogue. Whether you're writing a dialogue scene in a nonfiction narrative (such as a memoir or an autobiography) or a work of fiction (a novel or a short story), there are certain skills you need to develop if you're going to excel in this part of the writer's craft.

Think for a moment of a movie scene made up of great dialogue. We're thinking of one in Michael Mann's movie, *Heat* (1995). Robert de Niro and Al Pacino are sitting in a restaurant diner drinking coffee. Pacino is the cop. De Niro is the ruthless criminal. There is no action but the tension is as great as any action sequence you'll ever see.

How does the director achieve this? The answer is through great dialogue. There are pregnant pauses. Much is communicated through facial expressions and mannerisms - nods of the head, movements of the hands, frowning and leaning. What is said by both is brief. There are no unnecessary words. Every phrase and every sentence counts.

This is dialogue at its best. Here statements are like punches, exchanged over a table where a large bottle of tomato sauce stands, its vibrant blood red contrasting with the greys, whites, and blacks around it.

The only time the characters break from short exchanges is when one of them describes a recurring dream he's been having, about dead people who don't talk - a fitting and ironic commentary on the scene itself.

Genius!

It has no right to be this gripping - the scene is almost six minutes long - but it's acknowledged by those who know their movies as one of the most arresting and compelling dialogue set pieces ever filmed.

So what makes great dialogue? That's the question we want to address in this little book. This is not a work full of theory. This is a HOW TO manual in which we present our top ten tips to help you on your way to writing dialogue at its best.

We hope that by the end of it you'll be on your way to writing dialogue that's full of *heat*.

Happy writing!

Mark and Claire Stibbe

LET YOUR CHARACTERS SPEAK

One of the things most readers hate when they open a book is page upon page of narration, long paragraphs in which the author tells the reader about characters.

You know what we're talking about - never-ending paragraphs in which the narrator informs us about the feelings, thoughts, ideas, and back stories of the characters.

This is called *telling*.

It's not what most readers want today.

Readers in our generation are used to watching movies and TV programmes. In both you'll notice something pretty quickly - there is no telling. Directors don't have a narrator giving a voiceover, telling you everything you need to know about the philosophies and tragedies of the characters. These things are shown. They are conveyed gradually through the things characters do, the way they behave, through mannerisms and above all, the way characters speak and what they say.

Put simply, in today's world, *showing* is preferred.

If people want stories to be shown more than told, then dialogue becomes really important. So don't have large swathes of what are called "narrative summaries." Think of how you might transmit the same information more indirectly, visibly, and audibly, through what are called "immediate scenes."

When you write, imagine you are a movie screenplay writer or director. Ask how you would film what you're writing. If you can't film it, you probably need to rewrite it - and if you rewrite it, you almost certainly need to use dialogue.

So allow your characters to speak. Don't speak for them. Your narrator should not be intrusive. Narrators should generally speaking be as invisible as possible. Let the characters speak for themselves and in the process, let them live!

One more thing here: when you let your characters speak, make sure that they don't all speak in the same way. Write profiles for each of your characters before you start - profiles of their likes and dislikes, their ideas, passions, appearance, idiosyncrasies, relationships, backgrounds, and their strengths and weaknesses. Think about how each one would speak, given their profile. What tone of voice would they have? Would they have any stock phrases? If you didn't attribute a piece of dialogue to them, would we know from their idioms, accents and expressions which person was speaking?

So, in conclusion, don't have long stretches of narration without any direct speech. Create scenes where you tell the reader little and show the reader a lot. Your best way of showing what characters are like is through what they say. Don't let your narrator do all the talking. Let your characters speak, whether they are fictional or factual!

Apart from anything else, this is considerate. Your readers do not want to see dense forests of print on each page. They want the white light to break in.

Dialogue is white light.

It breaks into the forest.

It breaks up the page and makes the reading experience much more rewarding.

EXAMPLE

"I saw the surveillance video," Helen said, gripping an empty coffee cup with both hands. "I saw everything."

Ben slouched back in his chair and gave a shrug. He always had an answer. "What surveillance video?"

"At the bank."

Ben's eyes widened, chin jutting forward just a little. "What do you mean you saw it?"

"Detective Adams. He's got the tape."

"What did it show?"

"What do you think it showed, Ben?"

"I ... I don't know."

"A man in a blue hoodie. That's what it showed. A hoodie just like yours!"

EXERCISE

Although the dialogue may appear self-explanatory it's important to note that there is no intrusion by the narrator, no long winded sentences describing the scene and neither of the characters are speaking in the same tone. The author hasn't assigned accents, scene description or character description at this point, yet we get a flavour of what's going on without worrying about the rest. Ben may have robbed a bank; he may have stolen something. We don't know. All we know is that Helen is angry and Ben needs to do something about it.

QUESTIONS

What picture can you build of Ben from this dialogue?

What picture can you build of Helen?

What do you think Ben has done?

How is this conveyed to the reader?

CHAPTER 2

KEEP DIALOGUE TAGS SIMPLE

Dialogue tags are commonly known as "attributions". These are the statements a writer uses to attribute spoken words to various characters. They are the "he said"/"she replied," type statements.

There are three golden rules here:

GOLDEN RULE NO 1:

Try to write your dialogue scenes in such a way that you don't need to keep using attributions. Really experienced writers don't use attributions a lot. They make it obvious from the context who is speaking. If they are really good at their craft, they make it obvious by the distinctive ways in which characters speak.

Our advice is to try and reduce attributions to the minimum.

A good practice is to strip down your dialogue tags and then read your dialogue out loud to a friend.

Can they easily tell who is speaking?

As a matter of good practice, you shouldn't use dialogue tags in every exchange of speech but you also shouldn't go more than six or seven exchanges without using at least one.

So try and create dialogue scenes with as few attributions as possible.

GOLDEN RULE NO 2:

Do not fall into the bad habit of using complicated synonyms for "he said", "she said." Here is our A to Z of synonyms commonly and, in our view, often wrongly used:

A

acknowledged
admitted
agreed
announced
answered
argued
asked

B

barked
begged
bellowed
blustered
bragged

C

cajoled
complained
confessed
cried

D

demanded
denied

E

enquired
exclaimed
ejaculated

F

fumbled

G

gasped
giggled
gurgled

H

hinted
hissed
hollered
howled

I

inquired
interjected
interrupted

J

joked

L

laughed
lied

M

mumbled
muttered

N

nagged

P

pleaded

promised
purred

Q

questioned
quizzed

R

raged
remembered
remonstrated
replied
requested
roared

S

sang
screamed
screeched
shouted
sighed
snarled
sobbed

T

threatened

U

urged

V

vowed

W

warned

whimpered
whined
whispered
wondered

Y

yelled

Z

zaid (!)

Some of these should be avoided for the simple reason they are inappropriate.

"What a wonderful Chardonnay," the colonel giggled.

Words cannot be giggled.

They cannot be sighed, gurgled or smiled either.

Here's what we urge: don't use complicated alternatives to simple attributions. They draw attention to themselves and therefore distract the reader. They are also telltale indicators that this is a poorly crafted piece of dialogue.

So put the thesaurus back on the shelf.

"He said," "she said" is good.

Leaving them out altogether is better. You can do this by using beats (see chapter 4) or by simply writing the dialogue so well that your reader knows who's speaking from the context and from the way each character is speaking.

GOLDEN RULE NO 3:

Place your attributions early rather than late. In other words, identify who's speaking at the earliest opportunity, usually after the first completed clause in the sentence.

"I've told you before," his mother said. "Tidy your room. It's a thousand times worse than a stinking pigpen!"

That's the way to do it.

Don't frustrate the reader by leaving the attribution until the end of the mother's statement.

"I've told you before. Tidy your room. It's a thousand times worse than a stinking pigpen!" his mother said.

Readers want to know as soon as possible who is speaking.

EXAMPLE

Matt stood in front of the house, heart pounding in his chest. He always planned on being early, but somehow it never happened. Suddenly there she was, legs planted wide and a high chin.

"Where've you been?" Cindy said. "You weren't with Stan. I already checked."

"Pub." The word was out of his mouth before he could stop it. "I was down the pub."

"You're always down the pub. It's her isn't it?"

"Who?"

"You know who. The lead singer from Stone Cold Drunk. Oh, do stop gawping. I know a liar when I see one!"

EXERCISE

By 'showing' the actions and using attributions more sparingly, the dialogue becomes sharper and easier to read.

The dialogue is natural without having to be grammatically correct and gives us plenty of information about two people we have only just met.

QUESTIONS

What is Cindy accusing Matt of?

Who's doing all the talking and why?

How are attributions (dialogue tags) used here?

What effect does this have?

CHAPTER 3

USE PUNCTUATION CORRECTLY

Here are our top ten tips for punctuating your dialogue correctly.

1) When spoken words end with a full stop (period), question mark or exclamation mark, put these inside the quotation mark:

"He's not at home." (The full stop/period goes inside the quotation mark).

"Where is he?" (The question mark goes inside the quotation mark).

"You're crazy!" (The exclamation mark goes inside the quotation mark).

2) If you use a dialogue tag before spoken words, put a comma after the tag and before the spoken words begin.

His dad said, "That rat is still in the basement."

3) If you use a dialogue tag after the spoken words, the comma must go inside the quotation mark.

"She's drunk again," Billy said.

4) When the dialogue tag is a pronoun (he, she, they, etc), then you don't use capitals and you put a comma inside the quotation mark.

"The horse has bolted," she said.

5) When you want to give the impression of a piece of dialogue trailing away, just use three dots (called an ellipsis) inside the quotation mark.

"I just don't get why ..." Jim said.

6) When a person is interrupted or cut off in any way, use a dash inside the quotation marks.

"There's no need to be–"

"Don't you talk to me like that!"

7) When using a beat to break up a statement, use commas.

"If we don't get to him in time," Matt wiped his brow, "he will starve to death."

8) Always put the comma inside the quotation mark and before the dialogue tag.

"There is no point continuing," Jed said.

9) Do not use colons (:) and semi colons (;) in peoples' spoken words.

"The banks have been lax with lending; the economy is shot."

10) Use a dash whenever someone starts to say one thing but then decides to say another.

"It was frosty – hey, can I have a light?"

One final thing, if you're writing for American readers, then direct speech should be in double quotation marks ("), and any speech quoted within that should be in single quotation marks (').

"When I visited Jimmy, he told me, 'the postman left the package in the hallway'."

If you're writing for UK readers, you'll often find it's the other way round.

'When I visited Jimmy, he told me, "the postman left the package in the hallway".'

EXAMPLE:

Brother Lupo produced a semi-automatic from beneath his habit and casually held it out with two steady hands. "I'm going to ask you one more time. Give me the letter."

"No, no, wait!" David raised his hands and took a step back. "There must be some mistake."

"Mistake? You either have the letter or you don't."

"Well, I–"

"The letter!"

The monk wasn't kidding, not with a firm two-handed grip. David felt a tremor in his bowels and tried to swallow. "Please ..."

Brother Lupo shook his head. "You can plead all you want. I know where it is. Brother Angus said you were the last one to have it. His dying words were, 'David Lenox has the letter. Find him'."

"He was wrong," David sucked in a final breath, "I don't know where it is."

EXERCISE:

The above example shows punctuation for American readers. Here is the same dialogue and text for UK readers.

Brother Lupo produced a semi-automatic from beneath his habit and casually held it out with two steady hands. 'I'm going to ask you one more time. Give me the letter.'

'No, no, wait!' David raised his hands and took a step back. 'There must be some mistake.'

'Mistake? You either have the letter or you don't.'

'Well, I–'

'The letter!'

The monk wasn't kidding, not with a firm two-handed grip. David felt a tremor in his bowels and tried to swallow. 'Please ...'

Brother Lupo shook his head. 'You can plead all you want. I know where it is. Brother Angus said you were the last one to have it. His dying words were, "David Lenox has the letter. Find him".'

'He was wrong,' David sucked in a final breath, 'I don't know where it is.'

QUESTIONS

Do you see where the full stops/periods, exclamation marks and commas go?

Are they all inside the quotation marks and before the dialogue tags?

Can you determine what is direct speech and why?

Are there instances of speech quoted within direct speech? If so, why?

CHAPTER 4

INSERT VISIBLE BEATS

Beats are gestures or actions between statements. Instead of saying, *he said,* introduce a beat: *he wiped a bead of sweat from his brow.* These are ways of showing which character is speaking as well as revealing their emotion. They are switches from the ear to the eye.

Beats are the physical gestures, movements or actions that a writer can use between lines of speech. They are really useful alternatives to attributions ("he said"/"she said" statements). They are also devices that show rather than tell.

A) GESTURES

These often fall into two types: facial and manual. You can have a character raising an eyebrow before or after making a statement and use that instead of writing "he said"/"she said." You can present a character shaking her fist or tightening her grip on a pen. Think of different gestures that can be conveyed by faces and hands. These can be used as beats to interrupt the dialogue and convey the emotional state of speakers through showing rather than telling.

B) MOVEMENTS

Almost any kind of movement can be used as a beat (and as an alternative to an attribution). Think of movements that convey emotional states: one speaker moving closer towards another; one character lighting a cigarette or downing a glass of whisky; one character picking up a knife or a stone. There are many movements that can be used instead of an attribution. They can convey a lot about a character's internal state without ever resorting to TELLING.

Try this:

"You're out all the time. You're always on that bloody phone when you're here, texting her... always texting her. You can't stand me anymore."

Sarah lifted the drying up cloth to her reddening face.

"Just go. Just go... now!"

C) ACTIONS

You can create a beat through physical actions, provided they are consistent with the character. If someone says something and then throws a punch or hurls a pizza at the kitchen wall, that is a beat. It's a useful alternative to an attribution.

Watch a movie or a TV drama sometime and turn the sound off. See how much emotion is portrayed through gestures, movements and actions.

EXAMPLE

"Who's there?" The Governor let his hands brush the smooth surface of the wall and he caught a rare waft of perfume. He knew who it was but he enjoyed the game.

"Only me, dear heart." That sing-song voice. "We're almost to the living room. Put your glasses on."

"I'd really rather not." He shuffled into the living room and groped for a chair. "So much more fun in the dark."

"It's hardly dark, dear. It's ten o'clock in the morning. Oops! Here, I'll straighten that."

"What was that?" He patted the wall and caught the edge of a wooden frame through that tight squint of his.

He heard a scraping sound as she righted the thing. He just hoped it wasn't the Temeraire. According to the maid, his smoking jacket still bore a light dusting of orange from the last occasion.

"Only the Turner, dear."

EXERCISE

Underline or highlight the beats in this piece.

Make a note of what kind of beats these are, using the headings above (gestures, movements, actions).

QUESTIONS

How would you describe the Governor's wife?

What are the Governor's priorities or concerns?

How are beats used to make the dialogue more interesting?

How are beats used to reveal character?

CHAPTER 5

BE RUTHLESS WITH ADVERBS

Adverbs are words ending in LY. When we start out as writers we tend to use a lot of adverbs in dialogue, especially when we are told not to use synonyms for "he said," "she said."

Instead of saying things like, "he whispered," we say "he said softly."

Did you spot the adverb?

It is so tempting to opt for an adverb in these situations.

Example: "You're an idiot," he said angrily.

"You're an even bigger idiot," he replied furiously.

Adverbs should be used very sparingly. Try to make the tone of voice clear from both the context of what's being said and the content (word choice).

Here's how you could rewrite the exchange:

Example: "You blithering idiot!"

"At least I'm not a complete moron like you!"

See how the word choice conveys the tone?

Adverbs after attributions are usually evidence of poor dialogue writing.

"When you see an adverb, kill it," Mark Twain once said ... ruefully.

(We added the ruefully... it's called irony).

Another big reason why you should avoid using adverbs with your dialogue tags is because they are examples of TELLING when you should be SHOWING.

Example: "I'm not afraid of the knife," Bill said nonchalantly.

The adverb nonchalantly is the author TELLING the reader when he or she should be SHOWING.

Example: As Fred drew the serrated blade, Bill smiled. "You think I'm scared?"

All in all, remember what the great Stephen King said:

The road to hell is paved with adverbs

EXAMPLE:

Simpkins lay on his bunk, twanging the springs above his head. "Nelson," he said, mouth opening in a loud yawn. "You awake?"

"I bloody am now."

"Wanna play cards?"

"As a matter of fact I don't. I was having a nice dream about Marilyn until your horrible squeaky voice broke the romance."

Simpkins could hear that skinny mattress creaking like Nelson was moving about. He was probably combing his hair back like the spiv he was. "What was you doing? Having a bit of how's your father?"

"For your information, I was sipping a pineapple daiquiri on a beach in Hawaii. Incidentally, what did happen to that tin of pineapple chunks?"

Simpkins couldn't imagine his cellmate sipping a daiquiri in Hawaii. He was in for murder with no chance of parole. As for the pineapple chunks they were safely boarded up in a place only he knew. "It's in the wall. Behind my bed."

"Well, don't let me stop you."

Simpkins dropped his legs off the side of his bunk and made a beeline for his stash. And then he got to thinking. "How are we going to open it?"

EXERCISE

This piece tells us that Simpkins is in a bunk below Nelson in a prison cell. Again, we don't need much in the way of description, especially in the case of a prison cell.

The entire dialogue could have been rendered with a stack of adverbs where the above word choices clearly convey the tone and add a certain degree of entertainment.

Think of how you would describe Simpkins and Nelson and the pecking order in this cell.

QUESTIONS

What dialogue tactics are used to transmit this information?
How does avoiding adverbs improve the writing?

CHAPTER 6

REMOVE VERBAL TICS

In normal, everyday conversations, statements are full of verbal tics – "ers", "ums," "ahs", etc. Look at any transcript of a conversation and you'll see that this is so. Go people watching and listen to a conversation. How many "ers" and "ums" are there in a typical exchange?

Written dialogue is conversation with all the verbal tics, everyday pleasantries and boring platitudes taken out. Written dialogue is spoken conversation at its best, where every word counts.

An everyday conversation might proceed as follows:

"Hello, Claire," Mark said.

"Hi there, Mark. How are you doing?"

"Er... I'm doing fine."

"Um... What do you think of the weather?"

"It's a bit... er... overcast," Mark replied.

"Well, I'm still going out for a walk."

"Missing you already," Mark said.

This is downright boring. It is too like real speech, full of tics and banalities, platitudes and pleasantries.

Unless there is a compelling reason in your plot or characterization for characters to speak like this, avoid tics and other features of mundane, real-life conversations. Written dialogue is far more pithy and interesting. It reveals character and moves the story forward.

Try to remove anything in your dialogue that smacks of routine exchanges.

Dialogue should not read like a transcript of a real-life conversation.

EXAMPLE

"How do you plead?" the Judge said, peering over his bench.

Voices whispered in varying tones. The moment was here.

Bickerstaff paused, scratched his chin and stared at the ceiling. "Not guilty," he said. It was the better of the two options and the least expensive. Although ...

"Are you quite sure?" the Judge asked.

Bickerstaff took off his glasses and pondered the question. "Quite sure, Your Honour."

"But if I was to say there were witnesses in Walmart willing to testify to this misdemeanor, what would you say?"

"I would say ... they were mistaken, Your Honor."

"Walmart does have video surveillance, Mr. Bickerstaff. It would be wise to remember that. You were seen by Mr. Andrews, Mr. Prior and Miss Wallace seated here in my courtroom and all have testified to the fact. You were seen by shoppers ... children even ... masquerading as Adam, the first man. Yet you were found in Aisle 9, butt-naked and riding a child's bicycle. I think it's time you faced the music, don't you?"

Bickerstaff opened his mouth to say something and then changed his mind.

EXERCISE

Underline or highlight those places where a writer might have inserted a verbal tic.

QUESTIONS

What dialogue tactics are used instead of verbal tics in this exchange?

CHAPTER 7

MAKE EVERY STATEMENT COUNT

Every word counts in written dialogue. There's no rambling, no unnecessary words, no banal exchanges. Written dialogue is lean and often mean. It is at its best when, like the example from Heat in our introduction, statements are brief and adversarial.

This immediately distinguishes dialogue from everyday conversations. We guarantee that if a transcript was made of your next long conversation, there would be loads of verbal tics and a lot - yes, we mean a lot - of unnecessary words.

In written dialogue, there must be no redundant or pointless words. Your readers don't want direct speech to be like it is in real life. They want talk that propels the story.

So make sure what characters say is important. If it doesn't reveal something significant about their personality and if it doesn't advance the plot, remove or change it.

Dialogue that contains merely trivial comments ("the sun is out") or mundane pleasantries ("How are you today?") is boring and lacks heft. The comments may be brief but they lack content and conflict.

Here are three ways you can prune your dialogue and make every word count.

Have your characters use:

A) STACCATO

Short, snappy phrases are great. You don't have to have characters speaking in complete sentences.

Example:

"How's your sister?"

"Pregnant."

"You're kidding?"

"Due August."

"Who's the father?"

"Buddy of yours."

"No!"

"Yep!"

"We're screwed."

You see how effective that is? These statements are not complete sentences. They are staccato comments. There's a hint of pleasantries at the start, but after that it's quick fire, incisive and dramatic.

Often the key to this kind of dialogue is dropping words from statements. In the example above, instead of saying, "he's a buddy of yours," we wrote, "buddy of yours."

Try dropping words and see what effect it has. Make statements lean and mean.

B) SIDESTEPPING

Inexperienced authors tend to create dialogue in which simple back-and-forth exchanges take place. One character speaks and the next repeats something of what they have said like an echo, responding in a logical sequence.

Example:

"Good morning, Delia. How did you sleep?"

"I slept like a baby, all night long."

"Do you feel refreshed?"

"Bright as a daisy, thank you."

The trouble with this is it's not only filled with pleasantries and platitudes, it's just not great dialogue. Great dialogue often has characters sidestepping questions.

Example:

"How did you sleep?"

"I closed my eyes and it just happened."

"Why are you so sarcastic?"

"I need a drink."

This is the opposite of the previous example. In the first example, we have a simple back-and-forth exchange in which each line responds directly to the previous line, sometimes repeating a word or phrase. In the second, one of the speakers sidesteps the question and just says they want a drink. Now, instead of drifting with little interest, the reader's curiosity is piqued. Something is going on beneath the surface here and we want to know what it is!

Your dialogue will be a lot stronger when you learn to sidestep the obvious.

Try using more oblique statements and non-sequiturs in dialogue and see what effect it has.

C) SILENCES

Sometimes what is not said is more powerful than what is said.

If one character says, "I love you," and the other is silent, that speaks volumes. Whenever a character refuses to answer a question or respond to a statement, their silence often communicates far more than anything they could have said.

What we are really talking about here is cultivating silence.

Hemingway does this brilliantly in the scene between mother

and son in the story "Soldier's Home."

This is a short story about a son returning home from Europe after World War 1. He finds that while much has changed in his own life, nothing seems to have changed in his town.

Note: his mother calls him Harold.

> *"I've worried about you so much, Harold," his mother went on. "I know the temptations you must have been exposed to. I know how weak men are. I know what your own dear grandfather, my own father, told us about the Civil War and I have prayed for you. I pray for you all day long, Harold."*
>
> *Krebs looked at the bacon fat hardening on the plate.*

Notice how Hemingway portrays Krebs' silence. There is no reply. The soldier simply stares at the food on his plate.

That silence says far more than spoken words ever could.

And it's a great example of SHOWING over TELLING.

So, in conclusion, make every word count. Less is best. Master the three tactics above: staccato, sidestepping and silence.

Readers want to experience your dialogue.

They don't want to study it.

EXAMPLE

Let's take a look at this first piece and compare it to the one below:

"What's going on?" Barbara said, winding down the window. She could see a haze of black smoke and the underside of a bus.

"It's a road block," said the police officer.

"I can see that, but what's happened?"

The officer leaned up against her car, one arm wrapped around his middle. "There's a school bus up there. It swerved off the road. Someone said it was a drunk driver."

"Are you hurt?"

"No, I'm fine. It's the children I'm worried about."

"What do you mean?"

"Don't worry. It's nothing."

"No, tell me!"

"It's really bad." He began to sob then. "We can't get them out."

EXERCISE

Here's the alternative.

"What's going on?" Barbara said, winding down the window. She could see a haze of black smoke and the underside of a bus.

"Road block," said the police officer.

"I can see that, but what's happened?"

The officer leaned up against her car, one arm wrapped around his middle. "School bus ... drunk driver."

"Are you hurt?"

"Children."

"What do you mean?"

"It's nothing –"

"No tell me!"

"It's bad ..." He began to sob then. "They can't get out."

QUESTIONS

How does the first piece come across?

And the second?

Which is more effective?

Why?

CHAPTER 8

DON'T WRITE LONG SPEECHES

The best dialogue is composed of pithy statements. Try not to have a character saying more than two or three sentences at a time. If a character has to deliver anything longer, then break it up with beats and interruptions. Verbal economy is essential in written dialogue.

At this point some of you may be asking, what about a lecture, address, broadcast or sermon? Is it permissible to write long chunks of dialogue in these instances?

The answer, we would say, is no. Just as a contemporary reader is often put off by long paragraphs of narration ("narrative summaries"), so they are equally often put off by long chunks of direct speech.

How, then, are long addresses conveyed in narrative?

The answer is, "with great subtlety." We encourage you to think of ways of having parts of the speech rather than the whole lecture/ address/sermon. Choose the highlights - the opening, something arresting from the middle, and the ending.

Choose a point of view through which to observe and hear the address - one which permits you to insert beats easily.

For example, having a political address observed and heard through the sites of a sniper rifle allows plenty of beats!

And it also increases drama and tension.

Having a sermon observed and heard by a character in the pew is helpful too. They can look around at other members of the congregation while the sermon is progressing, looking at humorous details.

Any kind of what's often referred to as "speechifying" needs usually to be split up into smaller chunks. This is particularly the case if you're describing someone giving a lecture. In this situation it is tempting for inexperienced authors to let the speaker deliver the entire talk without beats or interruptions - in fact, without anything to make an academic and erudite exposition more interesting to the reader.

You must think of creative ways of keeping dialogue as brief and engaging as possible. In real life we don't talk to each other in long speeches. This only happens at special occasions - church, political rallies, academic lectures, after dinner speeches and so on.

If you find that you can't break the speech up without it becoming contrived (you can only take so much frowning, yawning, sighing, and other beats, after all), then write a brief narrative summary of the longest part of the speech. But remember, when you do this, it is very difficult not to move into TELLING when you should be SHOWING. You need to ask, "How would I film this?"

And that brings us to a movie, *The King's Speech*. This is the exception to the rule. The entire story of the film builds up to the speech the King delivers in the final minutes. Here the drama and suspense revolve around one simple question: "Will the King be able to overcome his stammer and deliver a rallying speech to the nation as war breaks out?"

In this kind of storytelling, a longer speech is allowed. It is completely justified by the plot. It is the entire point and indeed endgame of the movie.

But even in this case, note something important.

The director refuses to give us a single headshot of the King delivering his speech.

There are dramatic pauses.

There are many interesting beats.

There are shots of the voice coach (Logue) and of British citizens all over the country sitting and listening with rapt attention to their wirelesses.

So even here, the director breaks the speech up.

Look at the screenplay of this scene below. What can you learn about how to portray longer speeches?

KING'S SPEECH: Final Address

INT. KING'S STUDY/BROADCAST ROOM, BUCKINGHAM PALACE - DAY

Bertie and Logue stare at each other. Logue smiles, perfectly calm, totally confident in the man he's worked with. His confidence is contagious.

Bertie takes a deep breath, lets it out slowly. His throat muscles relax, his hands steady - all the things he's practiced.

BERTIE:

In this grave hour, perhaps the most fateful in our history, I send to every household of my peoples, both at home and overseas this message spoken with the same depth of feeling for each one of you as if I were able to cross your threshold and speak to you myself. His cadence is slow and measured, not flawless, but he does not stop.

INT - STATE ROOMS - DAY

In the listening room: Elizabeth grasps the sides of her chair and then slowly relaxes as Bertie's calm, measured voice comes over the speakers.

INT./EXT. MONTAGE OF VARIOUS LOCATIONS

The assembled dignitaries at Buckingham Palace, Myrtle with two of the boys, people listening to radios in homes, pubs, factories. A group of soldiers, including Antony Logue. Queen Mary sitting in her State Apartments, David and Wallis listening dolefully in a villa in the South of France, the crowds assembled outside Buckingham Palace, listening on loud speakers. Cutting continually back to Bertie as he grows in confidence

BERTIE (V.O. ON RADIO)

For the second time in the lives of most of us we are at war. Over and over again we have tried to find a peaceful way out of the differences between ourselves and those who are now our enemies. But it has been in vain. We have been forced into a conflict. For we are called, with our allies, to meet the challenge of a principle which, if it were to prevail, would be fatal to any civilized order in the world. Such a principle, stripped of all disguise, is surely the mere primitive doctrine that might is right. For the sake of all that we ourselves hold dear, and of the world's order and peace, it is unthinkable that we should refuse to meet the challenge. It is to this high purpose that I now call my people at home and my peoples across the seas, who will make our cause their own. I ask them to stand calm and firm, and united in this time of trial. The task will be hard. There may be dark days ahead, and war can no longer be confined to the battlefield. But we can only do the right as we see the right and reverently commit our cause to God.

INT. BROADCASTING BOOTH, BUCKINGHAM PALACE - CONTINUOUS

Bertie, in his quiet way is totally in command, and utterly magnificent. Everyone in the room is awed as he concludes:

BERTIE (CONT'D)

If one and all we keep resolutely faithful to it, then, with God's help, we shall prevail.

INT. STATE ROOMS, BUCKINGHAM PALACE - CONTINUOUS

In the listening room we see the elated faces of Elizabeth, Churchill, Lang.

INT. CONTROL ROOM, BBC BROADCASTING HOUSE - DAY

Technicians break in to spontaneous applause.

INT. BROADCASTING BOOTH, BUCKINGHAM PALACE - CONTINUOUS

Lionel and Bertie stare at each other.

LIONEL:

That was very good, Bertie.

Lionel closes the window.

LIONEL (CONT'D):

You still stammered on the "w".

BERTIE: Had to throw in a few so they knew it was me.

EXAMPLE

Hatti tried to make out the bride through a blur of tears. All she could see was Richard tapping that wine glass with a ballpoint pen, shooting her a look now and then.

He said, "Jane Austen once said, 'it is a truth universally acknowledged that a single man in possession of a good fortune must be in want of a wife'."

Hatti felt the gorge rising in her stomach and looked around for an ice bucket. How many weddings had she been to where all the grooms started out with the same Jane Austen speech, pretending they'd written it themselves? She kicked off her sandals and smoothed down that taffeta skirt.

'Now much as I like to think I'm as handsome as Mr. Darcy,' Richard said, looking down at Sarah, 'and that alone establishes me as a man of good fortune, my only good fortune was when I met Sarah.'

A round of applause and a few stamping feet, all because poor bloody Sarah could no longer hide the eight month bulge in that wedding dress. "I think I'm going to be sick," Hatti said, wiping a slur of wine from her chin.

The groomsman on her right was nice looking. Will, he said his name was. And yes, he agreed, it was all a bit sick, Sarah marrying a merchant banker from Cirencester. Only he didn't say banker, he said another word and it made them both laugh.

"He ditched me for her," Hatti said, finger pointing in their general direction. She was crying now. "He ditched me ... Why?"

And then that same old drone ...

"She's certainly has a price beyond rubies and I'd like to thank my new father-in-law for making me the richest man in the world by letting me marry her."

That's when Hatti threw up.

EXERCISE

Here we see a bridesmaid struggling with several emotions and a few too many drinks. Underline or highlight those sentences and phrases that weave in and out of Richard's speech.

QUESTIONS

How has a potentially long piece of direct speech (a wedding speech) been made more interesting here?

How has its length been shortened and its impact increased?

What can you learn from this exercise about representing long speeches?

CHAPTER 9

NEVER ENGAGE
IN INFO DUMPING

One of the greatest challenges in writing stories is what's called "exposition." Exposition is when a writer inserts vital background information in a story.

If you've seen the *Austin Powers* movies, you'll have seen how this part of the storytelling art is parodied through the character played by actor, Michael York. His character is called "Basil Exposition" and his role is to provide background information to Austin Powers - information about the "plot", "plot" in the sense of the conspiracy perpetrated by Dr Evil (another deliberate send up), and "plot" in the sense of the storyline that the viewer is trying to follow.

Basil Exposition is a constant, comic reminder to all writers that there is a right way to convey background information and there's a wrong way too.

The wrong way is called "info dumping." This is when an inexperienced or incompetent writer clumsily and carelessly dumps background information into dialogue.

The reason "info dumping" doesn't work is because it always involves one character telling another character what that character already knows!

They are doing this for the reader (if it's a book) or the viewer (if it's a film).

They might just as well give an aside and address the reader directly, as in classical dramas. But this kind of tactic has long since been abandoned. It is old-fashioned TELLING rather than SHOWING.

Here's an example of "info dumping."

"Harold, your son Jamie, the vet who graduated last year with honours, is on the phone."

That is really poor writing, yet it is astonishing how often you see examples of it in even the most popular writing.

Harold knows that Jamie is his son. He also knows what his son's degree was and the year of his graduation.

The writer (us!) has simply dumped background info into a character's speech for the reader's benefit, not for the character's.

It's what we call, "As you know, Bill," dialogue.

So what's the positive alternative to info dumping? It's what's known as "incluing." Rather than give an exposition about a character's background in a narrative summary, or through info dumping in dialogue, the skilled writer inserts clues about a character's back story in stages. These subtle hints are contained in words spoken by the character, or words spoken to the character. These build up over time to form a portrait or profile in the reader's mind.

Do you see the difference?

Info dumping involves TELLING the reader everything about background info, through contrived dialogue or narrative summaries.

Incluing involves SHOWING the reader bits of background info through cleverly written dialogue and visible, immediate scenes (ones that are filmable).

Avoid info dumping. It is one of the worst sins you can commit as a writer.

Practice the elegant art of INCLUING instead. The ability to inclue back story is one skill that marks out an excellent from an average writer.

EXAMPLE

"I'm cold, mom," Ten said, wishing he'd worn a sweater under that gown. "Since we've moved from Hong Kong here to Michigan I've been freezing."

"You Ten Foot Tsu," she said, "You good boy. You never cold."

"So, how did you think it went?" he asked.

"I like hat," she said, pumping the tassel with a tiny fist. "Your papa be proud. He been gone ten years."

Her eyes watered then.

"Here, you have this?" he said, holding out his diploma.

"Va-le-dic-torian," she said without stumbling and cradling the little scroll like it was a baby.

EXERCISE

Underline the phrases that look like info dumping in this dialogue. Remember, info dumping is when one character tells another character what that other character already knows.

QUESTIONS

How could you convey clues about the backgrounds of these characters without resorting to info dumping?

Rewrite the exchange in your own words.

And whatever you do, steer clear of the dump!

CHAPTER 10

AVOID WRITING PHONETICALLY

What we are talking about here is writing dialect in dialogue.

Sometimes you have a character from a region or a country and you want to convey the way they speak in their dialogue.

Be very careful with this.

Do not try and convey what they say phonetically - through going completely over the top in misspelling most if not all of their words in direct speech.

Here's an example:

"I bust out a-cryin en grab her up in my arms, en say, 'Oh, de po' little thing! De Lord God Amighty fogive po' ole Jim, kaze he never gwyne to fogive hisself as long's he live!' Oh she was plumb deef en dumb!" *

I wonder if you can guess where that's from!

It's annoying, isn't it?

Don't write like this! It is very distracting for the reader and slows up the reading process. Be careful that you don't draw more attention to how something is said than what's said

It is much better to use a word here and there that sends a clear signal that this person is speaking with an accent - from Mississippi (the southern drawl) or from North Yorkshire.

* *Huckleberry Finn* by Mark Twain

If a person is from a less privileged background, have them use the word "aint."

If they are from the higher floors of Downton Abbey, have them use words like "capital."

If they are from Scotland, just use the word "wee" here and there. Don't make their speech sound like a Robbie Burns poem (see below):

Address to a Haggis

Fair fa' your honest, sonsie face,
Great chieftain o the puddin'-race!
Aboon them a' ye tak your place,
Painch, tripe, or thairm:
Weel are ye worthy o' a grace
As lang's my arm.

Here's the translation!

Address to a Haggis

Fair and full is your honest, jolly face,
Great chieftain of the sausage race!
Above them all you take your place,
Stomach, tripe, or intestines:
Well are you worthy of a grace
As long as my arm.

Which would you prefer to read?

EXAMPLE

"So who's gonna ride in and marry me, little girl?" Bertha said, swinging that potato masher. "Because I ain't marrying up with just anybody."

She looked down at me with those big brown eyes and I knew she was mighty serious. My aunt Bertha's a God-fearing woman, but she big. And any man coming after her for a quick romp is about as dumb as a box of rocks.

"Who would you go with, Aunt Bertha," I said.

"If they don't come carrying a 'Federate flag, I won't go nowhere."

Her head seemed to tilt from side to side and then all of a sudden she closed them eyes and I watched to see if she'd fall over.

"You sleeping now, aunt Bertha?"

"No! I'm not sleeping!" she said, trying on a laugh for size. "I was just checking for holes in my eyelids."

EXERCISE

Notice how in writing this piece of dialogue we could emphasis the word 'I' and type it as 'Ah'. We could use 'ma' for 'me'. But this would only slow down the dialogue for the reader. We can hear the lilt and capture the sense just by the words the women are using. Adding more frills to the speech would spoil the flow.

QUESTIONS

Where do you think these women come from?

In what ways have we conveyed their dialect and hinted at their ethnic identities?

Would you have hinted at these things any differently?

LEARN A NEW LANGUAGE

Written dialogue is not our natural or native way of speaking. If you read really well crafted novels you'll see that dialogue is a superior form of everyday conversation. It is a language that needs to be learned because it is foreign to us. It is the semblance of speech more than actual speech.

In written dialogue, conversations need to flow quickly. There are few of the hesitations or pleasantries of everyday speech. Dialogue is DECLUTTERED conversation in which speakers cut to the chase. It is snappy, punchy and surprising. The best dialogue is confrontational, like a tennis rally.

The worst dialogue is too long, too similar to everyday speech (with pleasantries and tics), cluttered by complicated attributions, marred by incorrect punctuation, and above all full of the dumping of information which characters already know and is purely for the reader's benefit.

Our advice is to strip the dialogue in your first draft and strip it right back to its bare essentials. Then read it out loud to yourself and to someone else and see if it sounds natural and interesting. If it doesn't, subject it to further pruning until it is right.

Finally, when you have mastered all our top ten examples of best practice, learn the art of "multi-layered dialogue." Great dialogue is, at its best, multi-layered. It is often "multi-storey", or "multi-story." It has a rich, multi-layered texture, with plenty of subtext.

In other words, more is being said than the characters know or are saying.

Graduate towards the kind of dialogue we showed you in the scene from *Heat,* where the recurring dreams the two men describe hint at what is really going on at the table and what will eventually happen in the story.

Now that's what we are talking about!

HAPPY WRITING!

The Writing Twins

Mark and Claire Stibbe

www.ingramcontent.com/pod-product-compliance
Lightning Source LLC
Chambersburg PA
CBHW071123280526
45787CB00003B/1147